Exploring
South America

Continents of the World Geography Series

By
MICHAEL KRAMME, Ph.D.

COPYRIGHT © 2002 Mark Twain Media, Inc.

ISBN 1-58037-221-X

Printing No. CD-1567

Mark Twain Media, Inc., Publishers
Distributed by Carson-Dellosa Publishing Company, Inc.

Table of Contents

The Continents 1

Outline Map of South America 4

The Continent of South America 5

South America's Climate 7

South America's Resources and Industries 9

South America's Animal Life 11

The People of South America 13

The Inca Civilization 15

South American Culture 17

Brazil, Paraguay, and Uruguay 19

Colombia, Ecuador, and Venezuela 21

Argentina, Chile, Peru, and Bolivia 23

Guyana, French Guiana, and Suriname 25

South America's Islands 27

Answer Keys 28

Bibliography 30

The Continents

A continent is a large land-mass completely or mostly surrounded by water. Geographers list seven continents: North America, South America, Europe, Asia, Africa, Australia, and Antarctica. Greenland and the India-Pakistan area are sometimes referred to as "subcontinents." Madagascar and the Seychelles Islands are often called "microcontinents." The island groups in the Pacific Ocean are called "Oceania," but they are not considered a continent.

The continents make up just over 29 percent of the earth's surface. They occupy about 57,100,000 square miles (148,000,000 sq. km). More than 65 percent of the land area is in the Northern Hemisphere.

The Continents Today

HOW WERE THE CONTINENTS FORMED?

For many years, Europeans believed the continents were formed by a catastrophe or series of catastrophes, such as floods, earthquakes, and volcanoes. In 1596, a Dutch mapmaker, Abraham Ortelius, noted that the Americas' eastern coasts and the western coasts of Europe and Africa looked as if they fit together. He proposed that once they had been joined but later were torn apart.

Many years later, a German named Alfred Lothar Wegener published a book in which he explained his theory of the "**Continental Drift**." Wegener, like Ortelius, believed that the earth originally had been one super continent. He named it **Pangaea** from the Greek word meaning "all lands." He believed that the large landmass was a lighter rock that floated on a heavier rock, like ice floats on water.

Wegener's theory stated that the landmasses were still moving at a rate of about one yard each century. Wegener believed that Pangaea existed in the Permian Age. Then Pangaea slowly divided into two continents, the upper part, **Laurasia**, and the lower, **Gondwanaland**, during the Triassic Age.

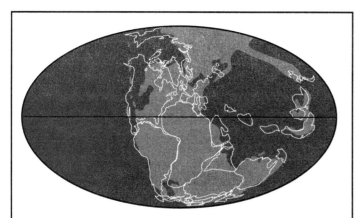

Wegener's theoretical continent, Pangaea, during the Permian Age (white outlines indicate current continents)

1

By the Jurassic Age, the land-masses had moved into what we could recognize as the seven continents, although they were still located near each other. Eventually, the continents "drifted" to their present locations.

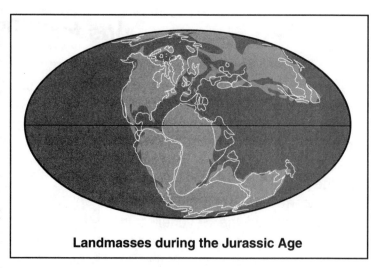

Landmasses during the Jurassic Age

Most scientists had been in agreement on the continental drift theory until researchers in the 1960s discovered several major mountain ranges on the ocean floor. These mountains suggested that the earth's crust consists of about 20 slabs or **plates**.

These discoveries led to a new theory, "**Plate Tectonics**," which has become more popular. This theory suggests that these plates move a few inches each year. In some places the plates are moving apart, while in others the plates are colliding or scraping against each other.

Scientists also discovered that most volcanoes and earthquakes occur along the boundaries of the various plates. They hope that further study will help them increase their understanding of Earth's story.

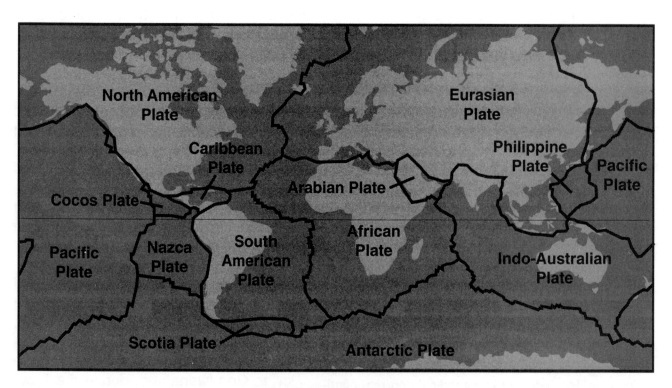

The Tectonic Plates

2

Name: _____ Date: _____

Questions for Consideration

1. What is a continent? _____

    _____

2. The continents make up what percentage of the earth's surface?

    _____

3. What was the name of Wegener's theory?

    _____

4. What is the name of the newer theory that replaced Wegener's?

    _____

5. What two natural happenings occur near the boundaries of the plates?

    _____

Map Project

On the map below, label all seven of the continents.

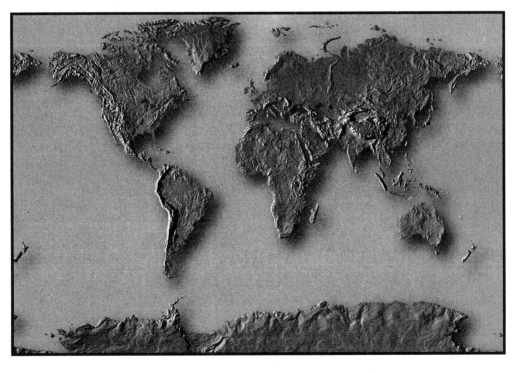

Name: _____   Date: _____

Outline Map of South America

The Continent of South America

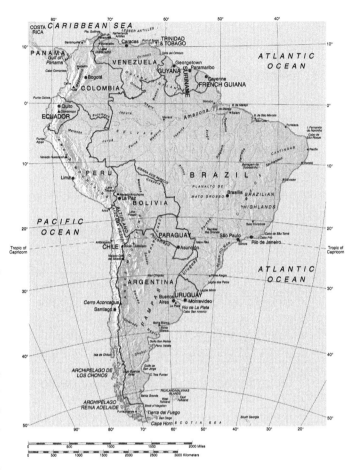

South America is the fourth-largest of the seven continents. It covers about 6,880,800 square miles (17,821,000 sq. km). It is almost 4,600 miles (7,400 km) long and about 3,200 miles (5,100 km) across at its widest point.

Most of South America is south of the equator. The Tropic of Capricorn nearly bisects the continent. Not only is the continent south of North America, but most of it lies farther east also. Lima, Peru, is one of South America's most western cities. Yet, it is farther east than Miami, Florida.

To the north, the continent is connected to Central and North America at the Isthmus of Panama. The northern border is on the Caribbean Sea and the Atlantic Ocean. The eastern border is on the Atlantic Ocean, and the western border is on the Pacific Ocean.

South America has many large plains and plateaus. These flatlands are used for farming and raising animal herds. The pampas is a fertile plain used by both farmers and ranchers. South America has some desert land as well.

The continent is also known for its vast rain forest areas, especially along the Amazon River basin. Ecologists are concerned about the large areas of rain forest lost each year to development.

The Amazon is South America's longest river and the world's second-longest river. It begins in the Andes Mountains of Peru and travels 4,050 miles (6,518 km) before it empties into the Atlantic Ocean on Brazil's coastline. Although it is not the world's longest river, the Amazon has more tributaries (other rivers and streams draining into it), drains more land, and has a greater volume of water than any other river. Other major South American rivers include the Paraná, Paraguay, and Uruguay Rivers.

South America has many spectacular waterfalls. Angel Falls in Argentina is the world's highest waterfall.

The Andes make up the world's longest mountain range. The range stretches about 4,500 miles (7,240 km) along the entire western side of South America. Many of the Andes peaks are over 20,000 feet (6,096 m) high. Only the Himalayas of Asia are higher. Aconcagua, in Argentina, is the Western Hemisphere's highest point. It is over 22,800 feet (6,950 m) above sea level.

South America does not have many large lakes. Maracaibo is the continent's largest lake. It covers over 6,300 square miles (16,300 sq. km). Titicaca is the world's highest navigable lake at an altitude of 12,500 feet (3,810 m). It is in the Andes on the border between Peru and Bolivia.

Name: _____ Date: _____

Questions for Consideration

1. What bisects South America?

   _____

2. What connects South America to Central and North America?

   _____

3. What is South America's longest river?

   _____

4. What is the world's highest waterfall?

   _____

5. What is the world's highest navigable lake?

   _____

Map Project

Using an atlas or globe and the outline map of South America (located on page 4), label and/or draw in the following:

Bodies of Water:

Amazon River

Atlantic Ocean

Caribbean Sea

Pacific Ocean

Land Features:

Andes Mountains

Equator

Isthmus of Panama

Tropic of Capricorn

DID YOU KNOW?

La Paz, Bolivia's capital, is the world's highest capital city. It is 12,000 feet (3,658 m) above sea level.

South America's Climate

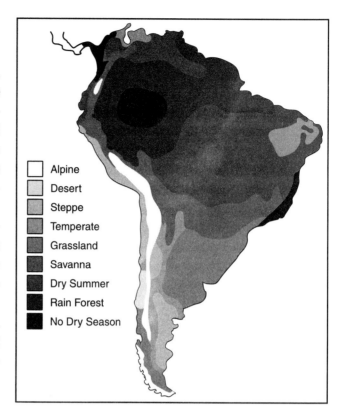

Alpine
Desert
Steppe
Temperate
Grassland
Savanna
Dry Summer
Rain Forest
No Dry Season

South America has a variety of climates. However, because of its location near the equator and the Tropic of Capricorn, the majority of the continent has warm to hot tropical climates. South of the Tropic of Capricorn are more moderate temperatures. This region has cool to cold winters and cool to warm summers.

Trade winds in the Southern Hemisphere blow from the southeast. Moisture from these winds are not blocked until they reach the Andes Mountains, so much of the continent receives large amounts of moisture.

The region near the equator has a **tropical** climate. Tropical climates have hot temperatures and heavy rainfalls. Most of the Amazon River basin and South America's rain forests are in this region.

Humid **subtropical** regions (also called **savannas**) of South America lie to the north and south of the tropical region. They include most of central and southern Brazil. In a subtropical region, rain falls on most days in the summer, but the region has a dry season during the winter months.

Desert climates of South America are located in parts of Argentina and along the coast of Peru and Chile. The Atacama Desert on the border between Peru and Chile is one of the world's driest places.

The highlands of South America and the Caribbean and Pacific coastal areas have a **steppe**, or semiarid, climate. These regions have hot summers, cold winters, and little rainfall. The largest steppe climate in South America is in Argentina.

Central Chile has a **Mediterranean** climate. It has warm and dry summers and mild and wet winters. Farther south, Chile's climate becomes what is known as a **marine** climate. The marine climate has milder summers than the Mediterranean climate and rainfall occurs year-round.

Highland climates are found in the Andes Mountains of Colombia, Ecuador, Peru, Bolivia, Argentina, and Chile. The temperatures vary according to the altitude of the region. The higher the altitude, the colder the temperatures become. Snow is common in the higher altitudes.

DID YOU KNOW?

In some parts of South America's Atacama Desert, no rainfall has ever been recorded.

Name: _____ Date: _____

Questions for Consideration

1. From what direction do the trade winds of South America blow?

   _____

2. What is the type of climate of the Amazon River basin?

   _____

3. What is another name for subtropical regions?

   _____

4. What is another name for a semiarid climate?

   _____

5. What temperatures do higher elevations usually have?

   _____

Climate Zones

Describe the main features of the following climates:

1. Tropical: _____

   _____

2. Subtropical: _____

   _____

3. Desert: _____

   _____

4. Steppe: _____

   _____

5. Highland: _____

   _____

South America's Resources and Industries

South America has a wide variety of industries and natural resources; however, there are still vast regions that have remained undeveloped.

While most of its resources are used for local consumption, South America is a major world exporter of coffee, copper, bauxite, fish meal, oil seed, petroleum, and petroleum products.

Its rich mineral deposits are located throughout the continent. The Incas discovered and mined gold deposits in the Andes Mountains centuries before the arrival of the first Europeans.

Throughout the centuries, the mountains of Peru and Bolivia have produced silver. More recently discovered minerals include bauxite, copper, iron ore, tin, lead, mercury, and zinc.

While South America has few coal deposits, it does have major deposits of petroleum and natural gas. Argentina has over half of South America's oil reserves. Petroleum and natural gas are the major sources of energy. Wood and charcoal provide energy for some of the manufacturing of iron and steel and the refinement of sugar.

The use of hydroelectric power is also common throughout the continent. It often accounts for between 40 and 60 percent of total energy use.

Most of South America's agricultural products remain on the continent. Many of the farmers in poorer regions raise just enough food for their own needs. Ranchers raise beef cattle for both home consumption and export. Some crops, such as bananas, coffee, cotton, and sugar, are raised to export.

While forests cover over half of South America, the continent has only a small lumber industry. Exports include only a small percent of the continent's wood and wood products production.

South America is almost completely surrounded by oceans, yet it has a small fishing industry. Most commercial fishing is for local consumption. Major fish harvests include anchovies, tuna, and crustaceans, such as crabs, lobsters, and shrimp.

South America's major industry is the processing of agricultural products. Other industries important to the economy include the processing of minerals and petroleum.

Important manufacturing products include beverages, electrical and mechanical equipment, motor vehicles, plastics, and textiles.

Name: _____ Date: _____

Questions for Consideration

1. Who first mined gold in the Andes Mountains?

   _____

2. Which two South American countries have long been a source of silver?

   _____

3. Which country has most of South America's petroleum reserves?

   _____

4. What percent of South America's energy is produced by hydroelectric sources?

   _____

5. What is South America's major industry?

   _____

Matching

Match the items in the first column with the correct examples in the second column.

A. Agricultural	_____ 1.	Anchovies
B. Energy	_____ 2.	Bauxite
C. Fishing	_____ 3.	Charcoal
D. Manufacturing	_____ 4.	Coffee
E. Minerals	_____ 5.	Hydroelectric
	_____ 6.	Natural gas
	_____ 7.	Plastics
	_____ 8.	Shrimp
	_____ 9.	Textiles
	_____ 10.	Zinc

DID YOU KNOW?

Alcohol made from sugar cane is a major source of automobile fuel in Brazil.

South America's Animal Life

South America has many common species of mammals, but it is the home to many unique ones as well.

Larger mammals are rare in South America. The continent is home to only one type of bear, the spectacled bear. Horses were not native to South America but were introduced by early Spanish settlers.

Some of the more interesting South American mammals include anteaters, armadillos, capybaras, chinchillas, marmosets, opossums, porcupines, sloths, and tapirs. Dolphins and manatees live in South America's coastal waters.

The Vicuña and Piranha

The continent also includes varieties of rats, mice, and bats. A unique bloodsucking bat lives on the continent.

South America is the home to many species of monkey. Howler monkeys and ringtail monkeys are unique to the continent.

Members of the cat family on the continent include jaguar, ocelot, and puma.

The South American llama, alpaca, and vicuña are related to the camel. Because the alpaca and llama are such sure-footed animals, they are an important means of transporting material on the steep slopes of the Andes Mountains.

South America is home to many varieties of freshwater fish. The piranha, a flesh-eating fish, is common in jungle waters. Other unusual species include flying fish and electric eels.

Over 2,700 species of birds live in South America. Flamingos, hawks, macaws, parrots, and parakeets inhabit the tropic regions. The harpy eagle is one of South America's more rare birds. The Humboldt penguin lives along some of the southern coastal areas. The largest flightless bird on the continent is the rhea, which is related to the ostrich. The largest bird capable of flight is the condor. Andean condors often have wingspans of over ten feet (3 m) and can fly at altitudes of over 25,000 feet (7,620 m).

A variety of reptiles lives in the jungle regions of South America. Boas, anacondas, iguanas, caimans, and crocodiles are found in many areas. The anaconda is the world's largest snake. It is a type of boa, sometimes growing to over 20 feet (6 m) in length.

The Galápagos Islands, located off the coast of Ecuador, are home to unique animals including Darwin finches, the Galápagos penguin, and the Galápagos tortoise. The Galápagos tortoise often grows to a weight of over 500 pounds (189 kg), and many live over 100 years.

Name: _____ Date: _____

Questions for Consideration

1. What is the only type of bear native to South America?

   _____

2. What two types of monkeys are unique to South America?

   _____

3. What flesh-eating fish lives in South America?

   _____

4. What is South America's largest flying bird?

   _____

5. What South American animal sometimes lives over 100 years?

   _____

> **DID YOU KNOW?**
>
> The llama was tamed by the Incas hundreds of years ago. In addition to being used to haul loads of up to 125 pounds, llamas also supply meat, milk, and wool to many natives of the Andes.

For Further Research

Choose one of the unusual animals mentioned in the narrative with which you are less familiar. Using at least two sources to help you, write a paragraph in the space below describing this animal.

_____

_____

_____

_____

_____

_____

_____

_____

_____

The People of South America

The heritage of South Americans may be Spanish or Portuguese, Native American, or a mix of both, Mestizo.

South America has a variety of ethnic groups. Major groups include Native Americans as well as descendants of the Spanish, Portuguese, and African settlers. Through the years, much mixing of the ethnic groups occurred. **Mestizo** is the name given to a large part of the population who are descended from the Native Americans, the Spanish, and the Portuguese.

Many of South America's natives are descendants of the ancient Inca civilization. The Incas lived mainly in the Andes Mountains. The Inca civilization flourished before the arrival of the Europeans. They had major cities and a road system of over 12,000 miles (19,312 km). They developed terrace farming and created large irrigation systems.

In the 1500s, Spanish soldiers, called **Conquistadors**, conquered much of the continent. The Conquistadors came in search of gold and other riches. They enslaved much of the native population and also brought slaves from Africa to work in the mines. The South American countries continued to be colonies of European nations until they achieved independence beginning in the early 1800s. The last nations to win independence were Guyana (British Guiana) in 1966 and Suriname (Dutch Guiana) in 1975.

Today, most of the Native Americans live in the highlands of the Andes Mountains. Spanish descendants are common in Argentina and Uruguay. Portuguese descendants are most common in Brazil. Many immigrants from other European countries later joined the early Spanish and Portuguese settlers.

South America's population continues to increase at a rapid rate. The population doubled between 1960 and 2000. About one-half of the total population lives in Brazil. Migration from the rural areas to cities continues to increase. In many of the South American countries, the urban population is over 80 percent. Most of South America's people live near the coasts, and very few inhabit the large central area of the continent.

Spanish is the official language of most of the continent, while Portuguese is the official language of Brazil. Other official languages include English in Guyana, Dutch in Suriname, and French in French Guiana. Many native languages are still spoken in the highlands of Bolivia, Chile, Paraguay, and Peru.

Over 90 percent of the population of South America is Roman Catholic. Members of both the Protestant and Jewish faiths also live throughout the continent.

Name: _____ Date: _____

Questions for Consideration

1. What name is given to descendants of Native Americans, the Spanish, and the Portuguese?

   _____

2. What ancient Native American civilization flourished in the Andes?

   _____

3. What were Spanish soldiers in South America called?

   _____

4. What is South America's largest religious group?

   _____

5. In which country does about one-half of South America's population live?

   _____

Matching

Match each country or region in the first column with the appropriate language in the second column.

_____ 1. Argentina

_____ 2. Bolivia

_____ 3. Brazil

_____ 4. French Guiana

_____ 5. Guyana

_____ 6. Highlands

_____ 7. Paraguay

_____ 8. Suriname

_____ 9. Uruguay

_____ 10. Venezuela

A. English

B. Dutch

C. French

D. Native

E. Portuguese

F. Spanish

DID YOU KNOW?

The population of South America is about 348 million. This is six percent of the world's population.

The Inca Civilization

The early history of the Incas is a mystery. Since the Incas never developed a system of writing, we must rely on the writings of their Spanish conquerors for any early Inca history. We can also study artifacts of the ancient cities for clues to the early Incas' story.

We do know some Inca myths. One early story is that the sun god created the first Inca, Manco Capac, and his sister. The god told them to go and teach other Indians. They went into the wilderness to establish a city. They named their city Cuzco, and it became the capital of the Inca Empire.

The Incas probably began as one of the many small tribes of the Andes Mountains. At its peak, the Inca Empire spread through parts of what are now Peru, Ecuador, Chile, Bolivia, and Argentina. The Inca land included desert, fertile valleys, some rain forests, and the Andes Mountains.

The Incas conquered most of their territory under the leadership of Pachacutec, who ruled from 1438 to 1471. The Incas crushed most of the other tribes during brutal fighting.

The Inca Empire was so large that a system of roads was built that stretched over 12,000 miles (19,312 km). The Incas did not use wheeled vehicles on their roads. The great road system was for pedestrians. Only the road system of the ancient Romans was equal to that of the Incas.

The Incas developed terrace farming. They cut terraces into the steep sides of the mountains to create more farmland. They also dug irrigation systems to bring water from the mountain streams to the terraces. Many of the Inca roads, terraces, and irrigation ditches are still in use today.

The llama was an important animal for the Incas. They tamed the llama and used it for transportation of people and materials. The llama also provided the Incas with wool and food.

The Incas developed a counting system that used a base of ten. They used a *quipu* to remember the numbers. The quipu had a main cord about two feet long. Many colored strings were tied to the main cord. Each string had knots tied in it. The color of the strings and the distance between the knots had special meaning.

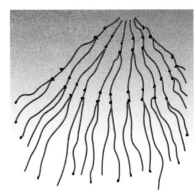

The Inca civilization was at its peak when the Spanish arrived. Francisco Pizarro led the Spanish invaders against the Incas. After a series of fierce battles, the Spanish defeated the Inca king, Atahualpa, and in 1533 he was killed. The descendants of the Incas continued to live under the rule of the Spanish until the various countries in which they lived became independent.

An Incan quipu

15

Name: _____ Date: _____

Questions for Consideration

1. What was the name of the capital of the Inca Empire? _____

2. How did the Incas grow crops on the mountains? _____

    _____

3. How was the llama beneficial to the Incas? _____

    _____

4. What was the name of the invention that the Incas used for counting? _____

5. Who defeated the Incas? _____

Map Project

The Inca Empire included parts of the countries that are now Peru, Ecuador, Chile, Bolivia, and Argentina. Using a globe, atlas, or map, label those countries on the map to the left, as well as the Caribbean Sea, Atlantic Ocean, and Pacific Ocean.

DID YOU KNOW?

The Incas were the first people to grow potatoes. Spanish explorers introduced the vegetable to Europe.

South American Culture

South American history and culture can be easily divided into three periods: native, colonial, and post-revolutionary.

Native populations lived throughout the continent. The most notable of the many tribes was the Incas of the Andes Mountains. Native arts included beautiful ceramics, textiles, and feather work, as well as gold and jewelry work.

The architecture of the ancient times included magnificent structures, such as those in the cities of Cuzco and Machu Piccu.

Performers often wear traditional costumes.

The colonial period began with the Spanish and Portuguese conquests in the sixteenth century. The colonial period is most noted for its architecture and religious art. Many beautiful paintings and stone carvings still adorn the beautiful churches and cathedrals throughout the continent.

Revolutions against the European rule began in the early 1800s. Soon most of South America's nations became independent.

In more modern times, literature increased in importance. Many South American authors became internationally famous. Nobel Prize winners include Pablo Neruda, Gabriel García Márquez, and Gabriela Mistral.

South America is a land of many festivals. These festivals are a combination of native and colonial, as well as religious celebrations. These festivals feature music, dance, food, and colorful costumes.

Music has long been an important part of South America's heritage. The native civilizations used a variety of drums and flutes to accompany several festivals. The Europeans introduced stringed instruments to the continent. The guitar, introduced by the Spanish, became a favorite instrument. Today's South American music is a blend of native, African, and European influences.

Dance has always been part of South American culture. In the twentieth century, several dances from Brazil, such as the tango, maxixe, samba, lambada, and bossa nova, gained international popularity.

Spanish is the official language of most of the South American countries. However, about half of the population speak Portuguese, the official language in Brazil. Other official languages include English in Guyana, Dutch in Suriname, and French in French Guiana. Minorities in many countries also use native languages.

Ninety percent of South America's people are Roman Catholic. Spanish and Portuguese conquerors brought the Roman Catholic faith to the continent. Most of the Protestants live in Brazil and Chile. The Jewish population lives mainly in cities throughout the continent.

Name: _____ Date: _____

Questions for Consideration

1. What are the three main periods of South American history and culture?

   _____

2. Name one of South America's ancient cities.

   _____

3. Which musical instrument introduced by the Spanish has become a favorite in South America?

   _____

4. Which country was the source of most twentieth-century popular South American dances?

   _____

5. South American festivals feature what elements?

   _____

Matching

Identify the term in the left column as one of the four categories from the right column.

_____ 1. Churches   A. Native

_____ 2. Cuzco   B. Colonial

_____ 3. Feather work   C. Author

_____ 4. Márquez   D. Dance

_____ 5. Maxixe

_____ 6. Mistral

_____ 7. Neruda

_____ 8. Samba

_____ 9. Stone carving

_____ 10. Tango

DID YOU KNOW?

One of South America's most famous festivals is Brazil's Carnival. It is celebrated throughout the country beginning on the Saturday before Ash Wednesday.

Brazil, Paraguay, and Uruguay

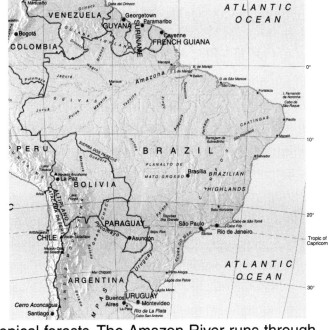

Brazil is South America's largest country. It is also its most populous. Over one-half of South America's population lives in Brazil. Most

of Brazil's people live within two hundred miles of the Atlantic Ocean coastline.

São Paulo is Brazil's largest city. It is the world's third-largest city. Only Tokyo and Mexico City are larger. Brazil's other large cities are Rio de Janeiro and its capital city, Brasília.

Much of the interior of Brazil contains tropical forests. The Amazon River runs through the heart of the country.

Brazil exports more sugar cane, bananas, and oranges than any other country. It also produces over one-third of the world's coffee. Other major exports include rubber, cacao, pineapples, lemons, rice, and cotton.

Brazil has large deposits of minerals and gemstones. However, it does not have major reserves of oil.

Paraguay is a landlocked country. However, it contains three major rivers, the Paraguay, the Paraná, and the Pilcomayo. The Paraná flows into the Atlantic Ocean, giving Paraguay a shipping outlet.

Asunción is Paraguay's capital and largest city. It is located where the Paraguay and Pilcomayo Rivers meet. The country of Argentina is just across the rivers from Asunción.

The Paraguay River also divides the country into eastern and western regions. The western region has over three-fifths of Paraguay's land and only five percent of its people. The harsh climate and poor transportation have hindered the development of the region. The eastern region has tropical forests and fertile grasslands. Major products of the region include cattle, coffee, cotton, and tobacco.

The capital and largest city of **Uruguay** is Montevideo. Most of Uruguay's land is grassland. This helps support large herds of cattle and sheep. Most of the nation's industry is related to raising and processing these herds. Meatpacking, wool, and textiles are of great importance to Uruguay's economy.

Less than ten percent of Uruguay's land is used for farming. Major crops include citrus fruits and grains. Flaxseed is an important crop, used in the manufacture of ink, linseed oil, and paint.

In recent years, tourism has continued to grow as an important part of Uruguay's economy. Many resorts are on its Atlantic Ocean coastline.

Name: _____ Date: _____

Questions for Consideration

1. What is Brazil's largest city?

   _____

2. Brazil exports more of what three products than any other country?

   _____

3. What are the three major rivers in Paraguay?

   _____

4. Flaxseed is used in the manufacture of what products?

   _____

5. What two animals are the most important to Uruguay's economy?

   _____

Map Project

On the map, label the following. The black dots indicate cities.

Asunción
Amazon River
Brasília
Brazil
Montevideo

Paraguay
Rio de Janeiro
São Paulo
Uruguay

DID YOU KNOW?

Most of the Amazon River runs through Brazil. It is both the world's widest and deepest river.

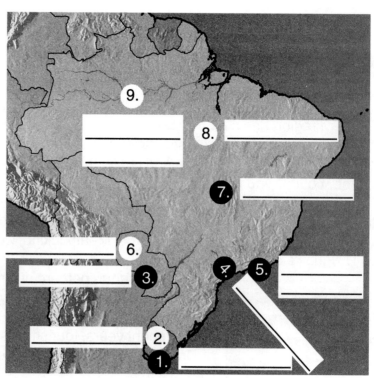

Colombia, Ecuador, and Venezuela

Colombia became independent from Spain in 1819. Bogotá is Colombia's capital and major industrial city.

Colombia's major industries include farming and mining. It does 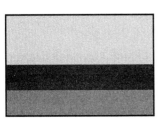 have petroleum resources but still has to import oil to meet its energy demands.

Colombia has the world's largest deposits of platinum. It also has major deposits of gold and emeralds. It supplies about 90 percent of the world's emeralds.

Coffee, cotton, corn, rice, potatoes, and sugar cane are major crops. About 80 percent of Colombia's export income is from coffee. Flowers are also raised for export.

Ecuador was once the northern part of the ancient Inca Empire. The Spanish conquered the region in 1533. Ecuador gained independence in 1822 and became part of Colombia. It separated from Colombia in 1830.

 The Andes Mountains cover about one-fourth of Ecuador's land area. The mountain region contains many mineral resources and is the site of much tourism. Quito, Ecuador's capital, is located in the Andes foothills.

The coastal plain contains rich farmland. Major crops grown for export include bananas, cacao, and coffee.

The eastern region of Ecuador contains tropical jungles. It is poorly developed. Deposits of petroleum were discovered in the 1960s, and today, petroleum accounts for about half of Ecuador's exports.

Venezuela has been a major producer of petroleum since the 1920s. Today, petroleum accounts for over 70 percent of the nation's income.

Venezuela's capital, Caracas, has many beautiful skyscrapers and homes. However, there are also major slum areas where people suffer from malnutrition and extreme poverty.

Raising cattle has been important to Venezuela's economy for many years. Recently,  because of irrigation projects, more of the country's land is becoming farmland.

Mining has also been an important part of Venezuela's economy. Miners have been extracting diamonds and iron ore for many years. Much of the iron ore was shipped to the United States to be made into steel.

Name: _____ Date: _____

Questions for Consideration

1. Colombia has the world's largest deposits of what metal?

   _____

2. Colombia provides 90 percent of the world's supply of what gemstone?

   _____

3. When did Ecuador separate from Colombia?

   _____

4. What percent of Venezuela's income comes from petroleum?

   _____

5. Where was most of Venezuela's iron ore shipped?

   _____

Map Project

On the map, label the following. The black dots indicate cities.

Colombia   Bogotá
Caribbean Sea   Caracas
Ecuador   Pacific Ocean
Venezuela   Quito

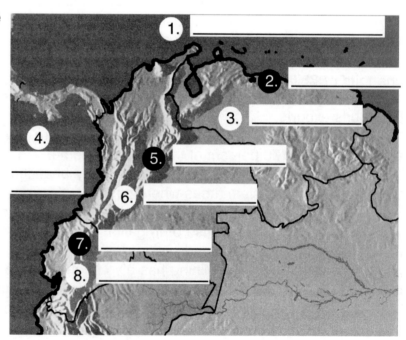

DID YOU KNOW?

Much of the world's illegal drug supply comes from Colombia. Many nations are working with Colombia to cut down on drug traffic.

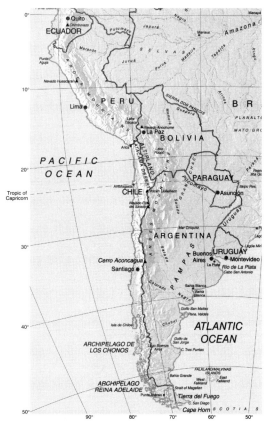

Argentina, Chile, Peru, and Bolivia

Argentina came under Spanish control in 1516. In 1816, the Spanish colonists gained independence.

Buenos Aires is Argentina's capital, largest city, and major port.

The northern part of Argentina is a subtropical region, the **Chaco**. It is mainly a forest region. Farther south, the **Pampas** grassland contains some of the world's most fertile soil. Major herds of livestock include cattle, sheep, and hogs. Major crops include alfalfa, corn, flax, soybeans, and wheat. Flax is used to make linen cloth. The southern part of Argentina is a high plain named **Patagonia**. It is a cold, dry, windy, sparsely populated region. The western border with Chile is in the Andes Mountains.

Chile is a long, narrow country along the Pacific Ocean coast. The northern region is primarily desert. The central valley of Chile has flat land and a mild climate where over three-fourths of the population lives. The Archipelago in the south

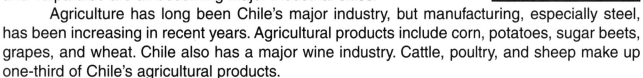

has few people and little farmland. It is made up of thousands of small islands.

Chile's capital and largest city is Santiago. Santiago, Concepción, and Valparaiso are all becoming major industrial cities.

Agriculture has long been Chile's major industry, but manufacturing, especially steel, has been increasing in recent years. Agricultural products include corn, potatoes, sugar beets, grapes, and wheat. Chile also has a major wine industry. Cattle, poultry, and sheep make up one-third of Chile's agricultural products.

Peru's capital and largest city is Lima. The country has three major regions: its coastal region, the Andes Mountains, and the plains at the base of the Andes. Peru's coastal waters help support a major fishing industry; anchovies are a major part of each year's fish harvest.

The Andes contain many valuable minerals, including copper, gold, iron ore, lead, silver, and zinc. The Andes foothills include rain forests and jungles. Many of Peru's native population live in the Andes foothills. In recent years, petroleum has been discovered in the region.

Bolivia is a landlocked country and has had less outside influence than many of the other South American countries. Much of the country is part of the Altiplano Plateau in the Andes, where approximately 40 percent of the population live. Agriculture is the major industry with potatoes, wheat, and a grain called *quinoa* grown on the Altiplano and bananas, cacao, coffee, and maize grown in the lowlands. Major exports include tin, tungsten, and silver. La Paz is Bolivia's capital.

Name: _____ Date: _____

Questions for Consideration

1. What is the name of the northern subtropical region of Argentina?

   _____

2. What are the Argentinian grasslands called?

   _____

3. In what region do three-fourths of Chile's people live?

   _____

4. What type of fish is the major part of Peru's annual fish harvest?

   _____

5. What crops are grown on Bolivia's Altiplano?

   _____

Map Project

On the map, label the following. The black dots indicate cities.

Argentina	Buenos Aires
Chile	Lima
Peru	Santiago
Bolivia	La Paz

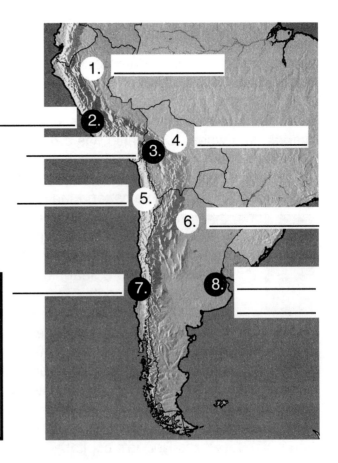

DID YOU KNOW?

Mount Aconcagua is the highest peak in the Western Hemisphere. It is located in the Andes Mountains in Argentina.

Guyana, French Guiana, and Suriname

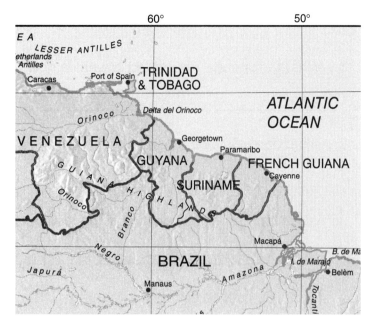

The Guianas are two small nations and a colony on the north central Atlantic Ocean coast of South America.

Guyana was first settled by the Dutch in the late 1500s. The British gained control in 1814 and named the colony Brit- 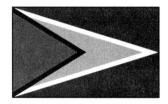 ish Guiana. It be- came an inde- pendent nation and changed its name to Guyana in 1966. Guyana means "land of many waters." In addition to its Atlantic Ocean coastline, Guyana has many rivers.

Both the Dutch and British established towns and large plantations. They also imported many slaves from Africa and Asia. Farming and mining are the nation's major industries. Major crops include cacao, coffee, citrus fruits, sugar cane, and rice. Guyana is also a source of diamonds, gold, bauxite, and manganese.

Guyana's capital, Georgetown, is on the Atlantic Ocean coast at the mouth of the Demerara River. It was named for England's King George III.

French Guiana is still a colony of France. French settlers came to the territory in 1604  and claimed it as a colony in 1667. About 90 percent of the nation's people live in the capital city, Cayenne.

Most of the population of French Guiana is descended from the many slaves imported in early years to work on the plantations. Most of the people live near the coast. However, tribes of Native Americans live in the rain forests of the country's interior.

French Guiana has rich, fertile soil. Farmers grow bananas, cacao, corn, rice, and sugar cane. Other industries include the mining of gold and the harvesting of timber.

Suriname (also spelled Surinam) was controlled alternately by the British and Dutch until it gained independence in 1975. From 1815 until independence, it was named Dutch Guiana. It went from a military to an elected government in 1988. Paramaribo is Suriname's capital and only major city.

 Suriname is a mountainous country, so most of its people live along the flat land at the coast. Almost half of the total population live in or near Paramaribo, the capital city.

Mining is Suriname's major industry. Ninety percent of its exports are bauxite and aluminum. Major crops include bananas, cacao, coffee, rice, and sugar cane. Its forests also supply lumber and wood products.

25

Name: _____ Date: _____

Questions for Consideration

1. What Europeans first settled in what is now Guyana?

    _____

2. What does *Guyana* mean?

    _____

3. When did French settlers first come to what is now French Guiana?

    _____

4. What two nations controlled what is now Suriname?

    _____

5. What was Suriname's name from 1815 until 1975?

    _____

Map Project

On the map, label the following. The black dots indicate cities.

French Guiana   Cayenne
Guyana   Georgetown
Suriname   Paramaribo
Atlantic Ocean

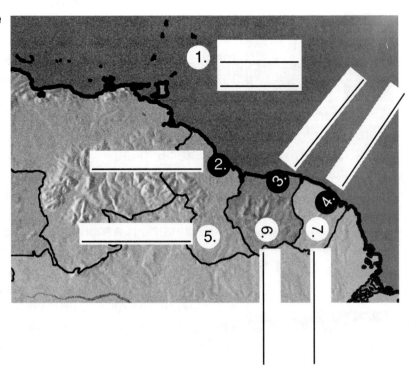

DID YOU KNOW?

Cayenne is a hot pepper. It was named after Cayenne, the capital of French Guiana.

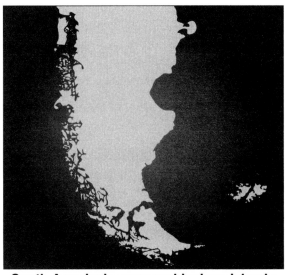
South America's many archipelago islands

South America's Islands

South America contains some of the world's most interesting islands.

The Archipelago includes thousands of islands off the coast of Chile. Few people live there because of poor transportation and a lack of land that is suitable for farming.

The Galápagos Islands are 600 miles (966 km) west of Ecuador. There are nine larger and about 50 smaller islands. They are located directly on the equator.

In 1835, Charles Darwin began his studies of the animals of the islands. He later wrote his famous book, *Origin of the Species,* based on some of his research while there.

Galápagos is the Spanish word for tortoise. Some of the tortoises of the islands weigh more than 500 pounds (189 kg). Other interesting island animals are seals and four-foot-long iguanas. Rare birds living there include pelicans, penguins, flightless cormorants, and albatrosses.

The islands are now national parks and wildlife sanctuaries. Anyone wishing to visit Galápagos must have official permission.

Galápagos tortoise

Easter Island is 2,350 miles (3,782 km) west of Chile. It is famous for more than 600 giant carved statues of people. The statues, called *moai,* are carved from single blocks of black stone. They range from about 11 feet to 30 feet (3 m to 9 m) high. Historians do not know much about the people who carved the statues or why they carved them. It is estimated that the last of the statues was carved before 1400.

Chile annexed the island in 1888. Today, just over 2,000 people live on the mysterious island.

Trinidad and Tobago are two islands located off the northeast coast of Venezuela. They are usually considered to be part of the Caribbean islands even though they are close to South America. They now form an independent republic.

Columbus visited Trinidad in 1498 during his third visit to the New World. Spanish and French settlers came during the 1500s. England controlled the islands from 1802 until 1962.

Petroleum, natural gas, and asphalt manufacturing have become the major industries. Both islands are known for a variety of colorful birds including egrets, herons, pink spoonbills, and scarlet ibises.

Easter Island moai

Answer Keys

THE CONTINENTS (page 3)
1. A large landmass completely or mostly surrounded by water
2. Just over 29 percent
3. Continental Drift
4. Plate Tectonics
5. Volcanoes and earthquakes

MAP PROJECT (page 3)
Teacher check map. Use the map on page 1 as a guide.

THE CONTINENT OF SOUTH AMERICA (page 6)
1. Tropic of Capricorn
2. Isthmus of Panama
3. Amazon River
4. Angel Falls (Argentina)
5. Titicaca

MAP PROJECT (page 6)
Teacher check. Use the map on page 5 as a guide.

SOUTH AMERICA'S CLIMATE (page 8)
1. From the southeast
2. Tropical
3. Savannas
4. Steppe
5. Colder

CLIMATE ZONES (page 8)
(Answers may vary.)
1. Tropical: hot temperatures, heavy rain
2. Subtropical: wet summer, dry winter
3. Desert: dry
4. Steppe: hot summer, cold winter, little rain
5. Highland: cold; snow in higher altitudes

SOUTH AMERICA'S RESOURCES AND INDUSTRIES (page 10)
1. The Incas
2. Bolivia and Peru
3. Argentina
4. Between 40 and 60 percent
5. Processing agricultural products

MATCHING (page 10)
1. C   2. E   3. B   4. A
5. B   6. B   7. D   8. C
9. D   10. E

SOUTH AMERICA'S ANIMAL LIFE (page 12)
1. Spectacled bear
2. Howler and ringtail monkeys
3. Piranha
4. Andean condor
5. Galápagos tortoise

THE PEOPLE OF SOUTH AMERICA (page 14)
1. Mestizos
2. The Incas
3. Conquistadors
4. Roman Catholic
5. Brazil

MATCHING (page 14)
1. F   2. F   3. E   4. C
5. A   6. D   7. F   8. B
9. F   10. F

THE INCA CIVILIZATION (page 16)
1. Cuzco
2. They cut terraces in the mountainsides and dug irrigation ditches.
3. It was used for transportation, wool, and food.
4. *Quipu*
5. The Spanish

MAP PROJECT (page 16)
Teacher check map. Use map on page 5 as a guide.

SOUTH AMERICAN CULTURE (page 18)
1. Native, colonial, post-revolutionary
2. Cuzco or Machu Piccu
3. The guitar
4. Brazil
5. Music, dance, food, and colorful costumes

MATCHING (page 18)
1. B   2. A   3. A   4. C
5. D   6. C   7. C   8. D
9. B   10. D

BRAZIL, PARAGUAY, AND URUGUAY (page 20)
1. São Paulo
2. Sugar cane, bananas, oranges
3. Paraguay, Paraná, Pilcomayo
4. Ink, linseed oil, paint
5. Cattle and sheep

MAP PROJECT (page 20)
1. Montevideo   6. Paraguay
2. Uruguay   7. Brasília
3. Asunción   8. Brazil
4. São Paulo   9. Amazon River
5. Rio de Janeiro

COLOMBIA, ECUADOR, AND VENEZUELA (page 22)
1. Platinum
2. Emeralds
3. 1830
4. Over 70 percent
5. The United States

MAP PROJECT (page 22)
1. Caribbean Sea   5. Bogotá
2. Caracas   6. Colombia
3. Venezuela   7. Quito
4. Pacific Ocean   8. Ecuador

ARGENTINA, CHILE, PERU, AND BOLIVIA (page 24)
1. The Chaco
2. Pampas
3. Central valley
4. Anchovies
5. Potatoes, wheat, and quinoa

MAP PROJECT (page 24)
1. Peru   5. Chile
2. Lima   6. Argentina
3. La Paz   7. Santiago
4. Bolivia   8. Buenos Aires

GUYANA, FRENCH GUIANA, AND SURNAME (page 26)
1. Dutch
2. Land of many waters
3. 1604
4. British and Dutch
5. Dutch Guiana

MAP PROJECT (page 26)
1. Atlantic Ocean   5. Guyana
2. Georgetown   6. Suriname
3. Paramaribo   7. French Guiana
4. Cayenne

Bibliography

Individual Books:

Kendall, Sarita. *The Incas.* New Discovery Books, 1992.

Kramme, Michael. *Mayan, Incan, and Aztec Civilizations.* Mark Twain Media/Carson-Dellosa Publishing Co., Inc., 1996.

Reynolds, Jan. *Amazon Basin: Vanishing Cultures.* Harcourt, Brace & Co., 1993.

Schwartz, David. *Yanomami: People of the Amazon.* Lee & Shepherd Books, 1995.

Shireman, Myrl. *South America.* Mark Twain Media/Carson-Dellosa Publishing Co., Inc., 1998.

Waterlow, Julia. *The Amazon.* Raintree Steck-Vaughn Pubs., 1994.

Specific Countries (series):

Cultures of the World (Series published by Benchmark Books). Each book was published between 1994 and 2001, contains 128 pages. Countries included: *Argentina, Bolivia, Chile, Colombia, Ecuador, Paraguay, Peru, Suriname, Trinidad and Tobago,* and *Venezuela.*

Major World Nations (Series published by Chelsea House). Each book was published between 1997 and 2001, contains 32 to 94 pages. Countries included: *Argentina, Bolivia, Brazil, Chile, Colombia, Ecuador, Guyana, Paraguay, Peru, Suriname, Trinidad and Tobago, Uruguay,* and *Venezuela.*

Enchantment of the World (Series published by Children's Press). Each book was published between 1999 and 2002, contains 44 to 48 pages. Countries included: *Argentina, Bolivia, Brazil, Chile, Colombia, Ecuador, Guiana, Paraguay, Peru, Uruguay,* and *Venezuela.*